ANIMAL QUIZ BOOK

By EDITH T. KUNHARDT
Illustrated by KELLY OECHSLI

A GOLDEN BOOK • NEW YORK
Western Publishing Company, Inc., Racine, Wisconsin 53404

Q: What animal lays eggs and has a bill and webbed feet like a duck, but has a flat tail and fur like a beaver?

A: The PLATYPUS. It uses its tail and webbed feet for swimming, and it uses its bill to dig up worms from stream bottoms. Its fur keeps the platypus warm.

Q: What kind of cat has no tail?

A: The MANX CAT has no tail. It also runs with a rabbitlike hop.

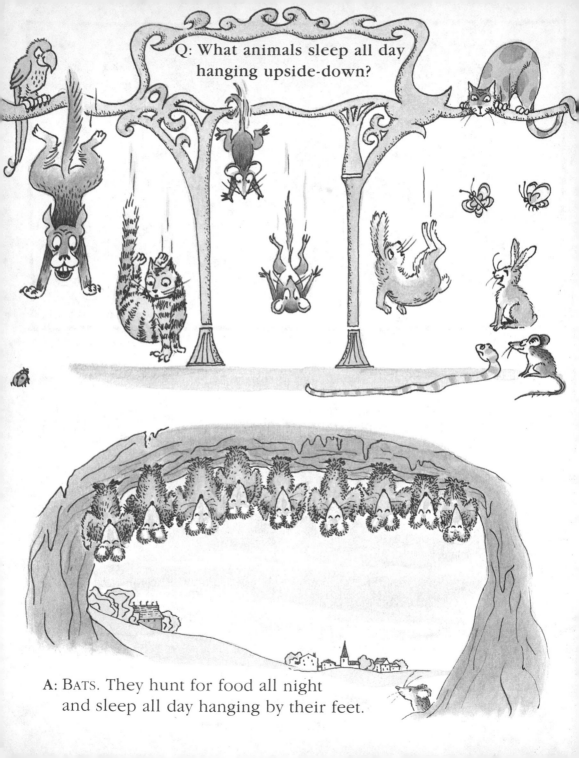

Q: What animals sleep all day hanging upside-down?

A: Bats. They hunt for food all night and sleep all day hanging by their feet.

Q: **What animal can swallow something wider than itself?**

A: The SNAKE. Most snakes can open their mouth wide enough to swallow things that are wider than their body.

Q: What animal can carry something fifty times
   heavier than its own body?

A: The ANT. Some ants carry huge loads of food many,
   many times heavier than their own weight.

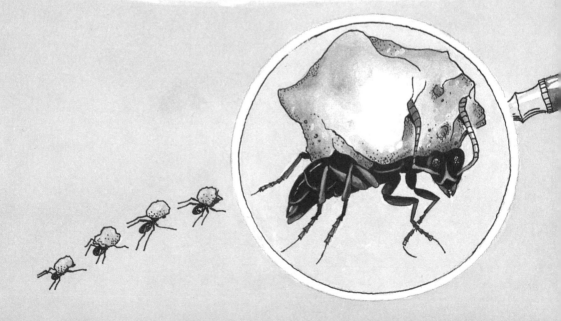

Q: What animal can change color?

A: The CHAMELEON. A kind of lizard, the chameleon changes color when the light or temperature around it changes. One minute it may be green or yellow, the next minute black or brown. It can also become spotted.

Q: What bird can fly backward?

A: The HUMMINGBIRD. It can also hover in midair.

Q: How does a beaver signal danger?

A: A beaver warns other beavers of danger by slapping its tail on the water.

Q: What is the largest animal in the world?

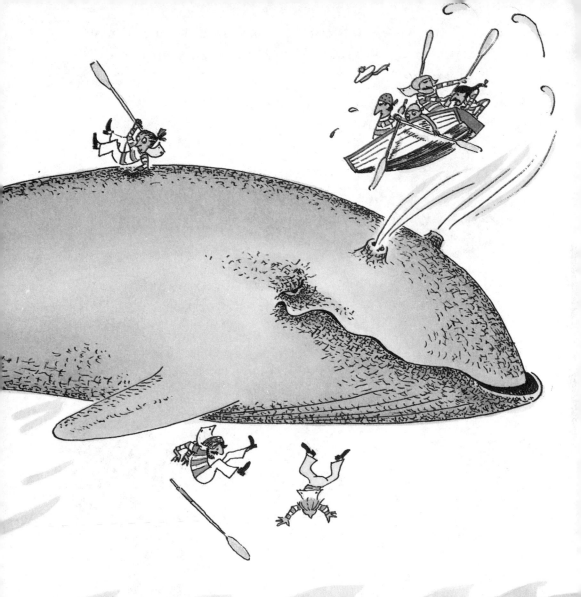

A: The BLUE WHALE. It is bigger than the biggest elephant, and bigger than the biggest dinosaur that ever lived.

Q: **What animal sometimes wears a "hat" to keep cool, and sucks up water with its nose?**

A: The ELEPHANT. Elephants sometimes put mud on top of their head to keep cool. They also suck up water with their trunk and then squirt it into their mouth or give themselves a shower with it.

Q: What animal carries its baby on its back when it swims?

A: The HIPPOPOTAMUS. Although it is a good swimmer when it is born, the baby hippo often rides on its mother's back in the water.

Q: What large animal builds nests in trees?
(Hint: It's not a bird!)

A: The GORILLA. Every night the wild gorilla builds a nest for sleeping, either in a tree or on the ground.

Q: What bird keeps its egg warm
   by holding it on top of its feet?

A: The EMPEROR PENGUIN. First the mother penguin lays the egg.
Then the father penguin keeps the egg warm in a fold of skin
just above his feet. He stands on the ice for two months, until
the egg hatches. He stands very still to save his energy, and
stays close to other father penguins to keep warm.

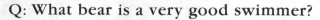

Q: What bear is a very good swimmer?

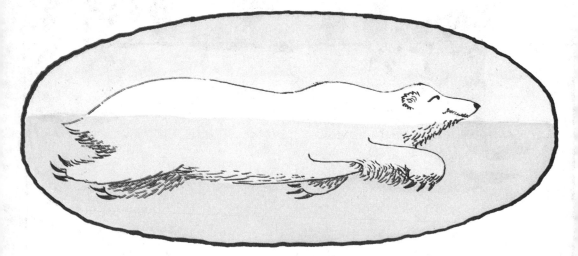

A: The POLAR BEAR. It paddles with its front legs and sometimes swims far out to sea.

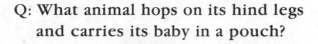

Q: What animal hops on its hind legs
and carries its baby in a pouch?

A: The KANGAROO.
The baby kangaroo,
called a joey,
rides in its
mother's pouch
until it is seven or
eight months old.

Q: What breed of dog was trained to rescue people?

A: The ST. BERNARD. In the past, it was trained to rescue people who were lost in snowstorms. With its keen sense of smell it could even find people who were buried under the snow.

Q: What animals live in "towns"?

A: PRAIRIE DOGS. They build their underground burrows close together, like houses in a town. Though they are relatives of squirrels, prairie dogs are called "dogs" because they warn each other of danger by barking.

Q: What animal can use its tail as an extra hand?

A: The SPIDER MONKEY can grab things with its tail. It also uses its tail to hold on to branches, so it can keep its hands free to feed itself.

Q: What animals wear special coats in the winter?
For the answer, turn the page.

A: The SNOWSHOE HARE, THE ERMINE, and some other animals that live in cold places grow white winter coats. With white fur (or feathers), these animals are hard to see against the snow, so they can hide more easily from their enemies.

Snowshoe hare

winter

summer

Ermine

summer

winter

Ptarmigan

winter

summer

Q: What animals build cities, wear special coats
and hats in winter, and have no tail?
The answer is on the next page.

A: PEOPLE! Humans are animals, too. We use tools to make and do things many other animals can't.